AN INSIDER'S GUIDE TO THE ART OF DEEP RELAXATION

JEFF KELTON, PhD

ISBN 9781086230147

To my parents,

who knew I was here to help others.

TABLE OF CONTENTS

PREFACE

I have been a long-term practitioner of clinical psychology, coaching, consulting and education spanning more than 40 years. As I reflect over my professional career, I have come to the conclusion that if there were only one thing you could do on a regular basis that would give you the healthiest and most productive outcome in your life, it would be the Art of Relaxation.

We all know that relaxation feels good and is important for staying healthy and coming up with our best ideas, but in this commonly stressful world with a million emails and information coming at us nonstop, etc. relaxed moments seem fewer and farther between. But what if I told you that relaxation was an art that can be practiced and expanded upon? That's where this book comes in. This book is a guide to the art of relaxation, to teach you skills and tools you can use to harness your ability to become relaxed.

Knowing how to relax is the most aligned and congruent way of being with the Universe. You can do no wrong by relaxing and there is no harm in it.

Knowing how to relax and committing to its regular practice is the key to a better life.

May this little volume help you use this key for relaxation to unlock your potential.

INTRODUCTION

Before I present these powerful ways to practice and benefit from relaxation, I want to share a story about how I came to this moment.

I had been traveling in India for the better part of a year and eventually found myself in Jaipur, Rajasthan. By the time I arrived, it had become brutally hot during the day, with temperatures reaching above 120 degrees Fahrenheit. It was pre monsoon and people who had the resources would flee to the hill stations for some respite.

Nighttime allowed for a lessening of the heat but was still uncomfortable, allowing only for a little relief from the mounting feverish conditions of the day. One night, I was outside of my room on the balcony hoping to catch a breeze that seldom came when I was suddenly visited by an insight that would set the course for my professional career.

Before I took off for India, I had completed an internship in clinical psychology at the VA Medical Center in NYC. Throughout my training, I had been puzzling over how to provide the best and most powerful ways to treat psychiatric conditions with the least amount of debilitating intrusions.

To put this in context, back then (late 1970's to 1980's), much of what was successful in the treatment of major psychiatric disorders such as schizophrenia, depression, and bipolar disorders to name a few, was grounded in a combination of cognitive behaviorally-oriented psychotherapy and medication. And the emphasis was on the use of drugs, which is still the case today.

But these approaches to treatment were problematic because the side effects of these medications were not pleasant. Even some of the behavioral interventions were less than kind. In extreme cases, doctors used more invasive and potentially debilitating therapies such as electroshock and brain surgery.

I was wondering what could be an effective way to treat these psychiatric conditions without resorting to interventions that could be damaging. So on that stifling hot night in India, I began to revisit this concern. All of a sudden, a light bulb in my head went off. It surprised me, because I wasn't sharp in my thinking in that moment. In fact, I was exhausted due to the lack of sleep from being in the stifling heat. Nevertheless, the visitation I experienced was like a jolt of electricity in its clarity and simplicity.

What I understood was that the one thing that could always be done in the face of just about anything, and especially with debilitating disturbances like anxiety, was to relax!

For many of you this may seem self-evident and I do believe we all can recognize how great it feels to be relaxed. Relaxing is a natural, biological process. It is like the air we breathe. It is a given. However, I think we take this for granted without considering the implications for why relaxation is so important.

What struck me was that relaxation was not only universal; it was also non-invasive. That is, it does no harm to the recipient of the experience. As such, the idea of relaxation fulfilled my desire to find an effective intervention for psychiatric conditions that was non-invasive and would do no harm.

Over thirty years later, this is even more true than in the past regarding much of what we do to heal ourselves. Furthermore, it has also been demonstrated how deep relaxation can contribute to a host of other benefits beyond health and wellness.

However, in order to claim these benefits, it is critical to know how to be really relaxed. The aim of this small volume is to provide the insights and suggestions for practice that will allow each of you to acquire a taste for deep relaxation. The experience of deep relaxation

is like a key to a magical kingdom. I invite you
to walk through this door!

Why Relax?

There is a growing body of research on the benefits of relaxation. It can sometimes be overwhelming to try and decipher what is claimed to be true and what is actually known, but there is consensus that relaxation can profoundly impact many areas of our lives. Scientific research on relaxation continues to be ground breaking, but going into detail about this research is not the intention of this guide. From my perspective, it is helpful to keep in mind the broad ways in which relaxation has been demonstrated to improve quality of life. To go deeper, I would encourage further investigation on your part.

Below are what I believe to be the major areas of benefit:

- Contributes to Healing
- Enhances Wellbeing
- Improves Performance
- Increases Creativity
- Reduces Conflict
- Reduces Stress
- Supports Spiritual and Transpersonal Work

From my personal experience both as a clinician and practitioner, I can attest to the promising directions that relaxation can lead.

With regard to health, there seems to be an overriding affect on toning down the extremes of how our physical body responds to living. It seems to help the body find its "sweet spot" and aids in a more efficient way of functioning. There is also a positive impact on how the body responds to illness and aids in lowering inflammation and improving immunity.

Wellbeing is enhanced since more of the body's resources are freed up and made available for other activities that can be more pleasurable and meaningful.

Even with respect to achieving results and maximizing performance, relaxation can help. This is particularly relevant to our culture's current emphasis on speed and goal attainment. Relaxation is one of the factors in finding "flow" and being "in the zone".

Regarding creativity, relaxation is the royal gateway to accessing those breakthrough insights so often treasured by artists and the like. Relaxation allows us to "incubate" and tap other, more marginalized resources, which can reveal new perspectives on problem solving.

It goes without saying that relaxation reduces the negative impact of stress on our lives. However, it can also help resolve conflicts, both internally and between others, which are great contributors to stress. My sense is that relaxation contributes to opening a larger frame of reference for different positions to be understood.

It is also my belief that ultimately, relaxation is in total alignment with spiritual and transpersonal concerns. These areas of life are underpinned by relaxation. Relaxation is fundamental to everything we do. To relax is to be One with the Universe.

DEFINING RELAXATION

Most attempts at defining relaxation do so by appealing to its opposite: tension. Relaxation is often defined as not being tense or stressed (lacking tension or free from stress). This approach is not very helpful and can even be misleading.

In my experience, relaxation is not static; it is a process. It is actually part of a bigger dynamic. When reacting to a situation, there are only two ways of responding: we tense or we let go – it's one or the other. This applies to all levels of human activity, even with emotions or thinking. And regardless of which action you employ, it is not static. It has an unfolding way about it.

When I initiate an action it is never all or none. It progresses. This can readily be demonstrated by borrowing from Progressive Relaxation Techniques, a popular way to produce relaxation that has served as a major application in many clinical settings.

Try the following:

Select one of your arms and raise it so that it is at chest level and then bend it at the elbow towards your body. Now, in whatever way you understand this, tense all the muscles in this arm and hold this tension for 10 seconds. At the end of 10 seconds drop the arm to your side and just notice what you experience.

Hopefully you will have noticed several things. For starts, it took an effort to keep the tension in the arm. Most attempts to use the muscles are not sustained for too long. Also the tensing of the muscles is quick. In contrast, when you decided to drop your arm there was an experience of releasing that was felt. For many of you, this could include the sensations of heaviness or warmth. There are other sensations that people report but these are the most common ones experienced. What is interesting is that the releasing continues for a long time. It can go on for minutes.

This little demonstration can be instructive in understanding the fundamental nature of relaxing. That is, the letting go is ongoing and is more like catching a wave rather than flipping a light switch. Furthermore, by staying awake to or aware of this letting go feeling, I can deepen the experience. Without this attention, the experience seems to dissipate. Actually, as long as I do not initiate another action to tense, the releasing continues.

So far I have been describing how relaxation is a process and that it is relatively experienced. I have also been suggesting that relaxation is foundational and serves as a fundamental building block to many other endeavors.

As a foundation, let's start with the physical, with our body. In order to clarify this and round out our understanding of what relaxation is we need to look at some ideas about how stress and relaxation operate on a biological level.

Built into our nervous system is a program for dealing with stressful events. Scientists have coined this the "Flight or Fight" response. More recently, some have added "Freeze" to the possible responses deployed. When this is triggered in us, the body mobilizes resources to manage the perceived threat. Muscles tighten or contract to prepare for danger, the heart rate rises and blood pressure shoots up. Non-essential functions such as immunity or digestion are not engaged. This type of readiness is regulated mainly by the sympathetic nervous system.

When we are free of danger, the nervous system shifts to what is called parasympathetic functioning. When this occurs, the heart rate slows down and the blood circulates more freely, the muscles release their tension, and food can be digested. It is the parasympathetic nervous system that is involved in what is referred to as "low physiological arousal". I like this term since it accurately describes what is going on.

When we are not stressed or fearing danger we are still engaged in a variety of activities that are necessary to keep us functioning as biological organisms.

We might say that this "low physiological arousal" state is what it means to be at rest. This is the preferred state of being for our biological organism. In other words, relaxation is never devoid of activity or arousal. Rather, the activity level that it is engaged in is within a context of functioning that allows for a broader range of resources to be available. Depending on what is needed, resources can be called forth as the situation demands. This is a condition of readiness as opposed to mobilization.

So I submit to you the following working definition of relaxation:

Relaxation is the cultivation of a low physiological arousal state that is sustained over a period of time.

As such, relaxation is the dynamic condition of the body that, when left to itself, is by default the natural way for it to be.

Relaxation is natural and the optimum state for us to be in.

The important implication for this is to be clear that relaxation as defined here is different from the type of "relaxing" associated with let's say drinking tea, watching a TV show that entertains us, reading a book, or even lounging on the sofa. Real relaxation has to be on a physical level that is sustained over time. Given the way we live in the world today, this natural state of relaxation is not a given and needs to be cultivated.

Let's turn our attention to how to develop such a skill.

TASTE OF RELAXATION

There are a multitude of techniques that can be employed to encourage relaxation. Several of these will be examined in the next section, but before launching oneself into some kind of practice it is good to have some idea of what it is that you actually want to experience. Fortunately, we don't have to go far to find what it feels like to really be relaxed. A few examples are listed below with some commentary.

The point to keep in mind is that as much as these activities can readily connect you to relaxing, the relaxation response is not dependent upon them. In other words, you don't have to have a good meal in order to relax. Instead, these activities are examples of high value opportunities to have the experience and can serve to familiarize yourself with what relaxing can be.

Having this taste of relaxation can guide you in using different techniques to relax more deeply. Regardless of where you acquire this taste of relaxation or what method you use to encourage relaxation, there is a basic principle that I want to emphasize and reinforce.

Relaxing is a process and progresses in its expression when attended to. In a very real sense it asks us to learn how to follow the flow. Relaxing is like catching a wave to surf. The wave can be big and have a lot of energy, in which case it is relatively easy to catch a ride. However, the wave may be a lot smaller and require a more subtle awareness to pick up how it is actually moving. In this case, the wave is less energetic and requires a bit more maneuvering to catch a ride. Regardless of how little or big the wave is, once you find it, it is just a matter of staying with it.

Some of the places where we can connect with the taste of relaxing in life are listed below:

- Going to Sleep
- After eating
- After Exercising
- Post Orgasm

GOING TO SLEEP

Actually, I hesitate having "going to sleep" on this list. Going to sleep should be a natural way to connect with relaxing. Biologically we need to rest the body on a regular basis. However, to simply lie down on a comfortable and supporting surface and close our eyes is not so straightforward. More and more people report difficulties doing this. To catch the taste of relaxing is not as easy as it may once have been.

Even if you are among the lucky who can hit the pillow and doze off, there are other challenges in recognizing the experience of relaxing. This is in part because we have developed habits that operate unconsciously to move us towards sleep. Despite these considerations, going to sleep is the only time in the course of the day that we deliberately allow ourselves to even entertain the idea of relaxing. This is when we are "supposed to" relax. This is when we give ourselves permission to relax. The total commitment to doing so increases the likelihood that relaxation may occur.

If we work hard physically, emotionally, or intellectually, the decision to cease all activities can readily yield to a relaxing process. However, even when the only condition for going to sleep is the normal schedule, there still exists a small wave of releasing that can be followed. So the possibility of having a taste for relaxation is available.

AFTER EATING

A great place to feel being relaxed is after a good meal. For proper digestion of food there is a shift towards greater parasympathetic nervous system functioning. And this shift is important to bringing about relaxation. There are also many acquired cues to prompt us to engage in a relaxing process. If we pay attention the sensations that accompany this are sufficiently strong to capture this wave.

AFTER EXERCISING AND POST ORGASM

On the higher end of intensity are the last two on the list: physical exercise and sex. These activities create bigger waves of relaxing. A great way to relax deeply is to build into your regular workouts a period immediately afterwards where you simply lie down and feel what is happening in your body. The wind down period can open you to the body's movement towards rest. For many this is an easy place to recall the taste of relaxing. This releasing is even stronger following orgasm. This is so strong that there are all kinds of descriptions from different cultures that note this. For example, the French have an expression describing the consequences of orgasm as the "petite mort" meaning "the little death".

To summarize, the idea here is to recognize the taste of relaxing and how it sets up a potential wave that you can catch. Sometimes just remembering such an experience is enough to shift you into relaxing.

THE WAY IN

There are a number of techniques or methods that can be applied to foster relaxation. My comments on these approaches will hopefully illustrate how each works to create a wave (small or large) of experience that leads to relaxation.

- Association
- Alternating Movement/Actions
- Pulsing/Slapping
- Vibrating
- Tracking
- Witnessing
- Tolerating
- Startle Response

ASSOCIATION

This is an idea that relates directly in some way to a feature of relaxing. This can be the use of a phrase or the conjuring of an image that is supposed to elicit the relaxation response.

One technique, called Autogenics, uses phrases like "I am heavy" or "I am light" often connected to a part of the body. For instance, a person would focus on feeling their right arm as they repeat the phrase "My right arm is heavy". They would proceed to do this with different parts of the body. Often this may be done in combination with other techniques. Using Progressive Relaxation procedures where you tense and then release a part of your body, you would also include the phrase as you release that part.

The use of association is also employed in visualization. The idea is to visualize a scene that is known, often a natural setting, to encourage relaxing. The difficulty with this is the reliance on visual imagery to bring forward the relaxation process. To realize the full potential of visualization requires the description of a place with all the senses involved and not just what you see.

So if we are visualizing a beach to feel relaxed, it becomes more vivid and real when I also describe the lapping of the waves, the smell of the air, the sensation of the sand beneath me, etc. The more senses included in the vision the more potent it becomes to elicit relaxing.

ALTERNATING MOVEMENT

The idea in this is that by engaging in a set of movements that are rhythmic, you can move into relaxing. There is an ebb and flow to how these movements occur. A good example of this is the practice of taijiquan (often referred to as Tai Chi). Here the practitioner moves through a series of positions that alternate between being closed and open. This is done in a deliberately slow manner. However, even the simpler idea of just swaying can induce relaxing.

PULSING/SLAPPING

This involves the energetic slapping of your body, sometimes very vigorously. This approach is incorporated in some types of Qi Gong exercises. The idea here is to stimulate the flow of the life force (Qi) to circulate throughout the body. The slapping brings the blood flow to the surface of the body and is clearly felt. This can be a strong wave to catch and ride towards relaxing. It feels like there is a buzz in the body.

VIBRATING

Sounding is very helpful in eliciting relaxation. This is particularly potent when humming sounds often found in various yogic mantras, "OM" or "AUM" being the most familiar. Actually any kind of sound made that vibrates in the nasal cavities will work. Making such sounds over a sufficient period of time sets in motion a vibratory cascade. This sounding feels like you are vibrating your whole head. I call this the Scramble Brains technique for relaxation. When this is done, even briefly, it interferes with normal cognitive functioning in such a way, that, for a brief period, you have no thoughts. For some this can be a very profound experience.

TRACKING

Other approaches utilize the way we can follow a process. I call this tracking since it is about observing what changes rather than keeping to only one thing. Basically you watch where the object of your focus is going. It can be as simple as watching the ever changing patterns of the clouds. A powerful way to explore this is described in an approach borrowed from Kum Nye practices from Tibetan Buddhism. [See APPENDIX on Following Sensations].

WITNESSING

This is similar to Tracking. The distinction I am making here is that in contrast to following a process you remain focused on a specific pattern. The pattern can be static or dynamic. When static, the pattern may be a familiar object like a vase. When dynamic it could be the breath. The idea is to remain focused on the pattern and nothing else. For many, this quickly gives rise to a sense of what might be described as boredom. However, there is an energetic here where such a focus can lead to a feeling of drowsiness. Once again there is a wave to be caught if you are awake to this.

TOLERATING

I refer to this as the Warrior's Way. The engagement of this approach is not so easy. Essentially you establish a posture that you stick to no matter what over a period of time. For example, you can choose to stand with your arms out to the side and parallel to the floor. In a few minutes this becomes difficult to maintain. Trying to maintain this brings into play a strong sense of your body straining which can then be released to in order to experience a strong relaxation wave. If one sticks with this there is even another layer to what can occur in how relaxation shows up. However, for the purposes of this book I am using this example to illustrate how to set in motion the feeling of relaxing. It is just another way in.

STARTLE RESPONSE

This last approach is very powerful and an advanced practice. As much as it is available for discovering the relaxation wave, it is not predictable and it requires the awareness to remember to catch the wave when it happens. Basically, it is the experience of being "caught off guard". This will happen, for instance, when you are totally focused on something that has fully absorbed your attention. Perhaps you have become immersed in a great read. Suddenly the phone rings and it startles you. For a split second there is this jolt of energy that runs through you. It's like being zapped by lightening. Too often when this happens we get thrown off and may react to being disturbed with anger, surprise, annoyance, etc. However, before you react there is a moment where you can ride the energy from being startled. The experience can be felt through your whole body like a seismic quake. If done correctly it can catapult you into a very deep state of relaxing.

The key to all of the approaches described is that each in its own way elicits a wave of experience that can be followed into relaxing. There are many ways to open the door to this experience. What is important to keep in mind is that this is the start. More is needed to really drop into deep relaxation.

PRACTICING RELAXATION

Hopefully by now you have the understanding that relaxation is not something you acquire by pressing a button. However, with regular practice the feeling of relaxation can manifest quickly. And what may have taken many minutes to show up can now appear in a matter of seconds. Thus, with dedicated practice, it is possible to experience relaxation "immediately".

Once initiated, the relaxation response can be deepened. If you allow yourself a sufficient amount of time to relax, this takes place. Staying in a state of what I have described previously as "low physiological arousal" has extraordinary healing and rejuvenating properties. Furthermore, every time you "dose" your self with relaxation it accumulates. It is like putting money in the bank. The more you relax the more impactful each session of relaxation can become.

In order to increase the benefits of practicing how to relax there are six conditions I would suggest you keep in mind. These are presented in a sequence of their occurrence.

SAFE GUARD YOUR ENVIRONMENT

Too often we forget to address this adequately. Your goal here is to insure that you will not be interfered with while practicing. Disturbances that occur in the middle of a relaxation session can be shocking and can negatively impact your experience.

It will help to find a place where you can be left alone. Put whatever form of phone you use in a no ringer mode or be silent. If you share a living space, put a sign on your door indicating you should not be disturbed.

As much as it is preferable to have a quiet space within which to practice, this may be unrealistic. Most people live in urban environments where there is a constant backdrop of ambient noises, occasional sirens from fire trucks and ambulances, traffic honking and so on. It may seem inviting that you use earplugs to block these sounds out, but I would caution against this. Part of practicing relaxation also contributes to strengthening your ability to ignore distractions. As you become more focused on the experience of letting go you will naturally block out most of the ambient sounds. Remember the idea is to minimize distractions where possible rather than totally eliminate them.

Besides the minimization of distractions, it is also helpful to practice in a place that is clean and tidy. Arrangement of flowers or plants as well as calming pictures can further set a desirable mood for practice. A lot has been written about what you can do regarding this.

In addition to managing the environment do not forget to be mindful of the clothing you wear. In general, they should be loose fitting especially around the waist. Make sure there are no labels that may irritate the surface of your skin. It is best to remove all sorts of jewelry. This may not be self-evident when you first sit down. However, as you ease into the session, things that you didn't notice come to the forefront of your awareness and then disturb your practice.

ESTABLISH A STABLE POSTURE

A great source of disturbance to practicing is our own posture. If I am frequently shifting my position I can never allow for the relaxing process to take hold and deepen. I need to figure out how to put my body in a position where once it is established I don't move from it during the session.

This can be a major challenge in its own right. It can be even heroic for some. Huge benefit can be gained by just struggling with this alone. Many may approach this from an attitude of force. They try to stay put out of a force of will. To maintain such a stance for any length of time is unsustainable. Even so, attempting to do this can still awaken you to the relaxation wave. I don't recommend this in the beginning when you are first developing a practice. [See Warrior Approach in THE WAY IN]

Putting aside the above considerations, I suggest being more gentle about doing this. There are three major body positions that are useful for this kind of practice: lying down, standing and sitting. Standing can be too demanding for most. Lying down can also have its drawbacks. Sitting would be the best for starting a practice.

Lying down is problematic since it encourages you to fall asleep. The brain interprets your lying down as the attempt to go to sleep. Of course, if you are in need of sleep than you should do so. However, the goal here is to cultivate an experience of relaxation while still remaining awake. Even sitting in a reclining chair is not desirable since the slide towards sleep is still encouraged.

Better to sit on a chair free of the back support. A stable posture to employ would consist of sitting up at the edge of the chair with both feet planted on the floor and your hands resting in your lap or on your thighs. The upright position will also aid in providing feedback to you when you feel you are drifting towards sleep. It does this by catching yourself tilting away from the upright position you established.

Keeping this simple, you want to be able to sit upright comfortably and keep as still as possible. Once you have set yourself up this way, you can further stabilize this by rocking from side to side a few times. Do this gently. This can help you settle into the posture more securely.

In other words, first establish your position grossly. Then with some slight movements refine this adjustment of your body.

For some, this way of sitting may be challenging due to various physical limitations. I know for myself there has been difficulty in this because of a congenital back issue. It takes time to cultivate a way to do this under such conditions. As a result, it may be easier in the beginning to use the back support of the chair to establish your stable sitting position. The main thing is not slump or to tilt your posture.

REVIEW YOUR INTENTION

Without proper motivation, most efforts to do something dissipate. Knowing why you want to do something increases the chances of following through with an action. As a regular part of practicing relaxation, it will be useful to review the reasons for doing so. The more relevant it is for you on a personal basis the more potent the intention will be. Remind yourself at the beginning of each session why you are practicing. Perhaps it is to improve health, better manage stress, become more creative, or connect to what is sacred. (See WHY RELAX). In reminding yourself of what your intention will be, make an effort to be very awake to what this means for you. Doing so will activate the whole of you to participate in the experience.

ADJUST THE BREATH

Once we have settled into a stable position and affirmed our reasons for practicing relaxation, we can now begin. I suggest you take at least three deep breaths. These should not be forced. It should also be done slowly. Attempt to breath from your belly (i.e., the abdominal area). Most of us tend to breath from our chests. This is often the result of constricting our selves unconsciously in order to brace our selves against the incessant occurrence of stressors in the environment. It may help in the beginning to place our hands over our belly so that we can actually feel how this area moves in and out as we breathe. Taking the three breaths is a way to demarcate the shift of action from being related to our surroundings to focusing on what is inside.

DO THE PRACTICE

This is where you follow the instructions of the technique you have chosen to work with.

A detailed guide to one approach (Body Scan Relaxation) is provided in the next section.

The length of time you actually practice should be limited. I suggest you start small and only attempt this for 5 or 10 minutes. As you get comfortable with the process, you can incrementally add more time to subsequent sessions. Generally I would aim to practice for 20 minutes at least once a day. You could expand this even more, but the 20 minutes is very productive. Time permitting, you could do this twice a day: first in the morning upon arising and then perhaps in the late afternoon or early evening. Personally, I regularly commit to sitting in the morning. Doing so allows for remembering the experience at other times in the day.

Many beginning practitioners worry about setting the time frame. Setting a timer or an alarm clock can be very unsettling and can startle you. If you aren't prepared to handle such a shock it could destroy all that you gained from the practice. I would recommend that you place a clock in front of where you are sitting that you can clearly read. Then I would go about your practice and when you think you are done gently open your eyes slightly, almost like you are squinting. It is kind of like sneaking a peak. If you need more time just close your eyes again and continue practicing. At first, you may find you are opening your eyes several times. Over time, you will eventually be able to open your eyes at the right moment.

COMPLETING WITH GRATITUDE

Once you have finished your practice, it is useful to pause before you actually get up to meet the day. After opening my eyes I take a few moments just to sit and allow myself to feel reconnected to the place I am in. Coupled with this I take note of what I have just accomplished and congratulate myself for spending time with my body. I then give thanks to all the sources of teaching and wisdom I have received about living a better life and that my relaxation practice will be of benefit for the whole planet. This is a moment to be grateful for being alive!

Body Scan Relaxation

Breathe deeply about three times and slowly relax your whole body. Relax your eyes, closing them, and let your mouth fall open. Let tension slip away from your forehead and scalp. Slowly sense every part of your head – your nose, your ears, your jaw, the inside of your mouth, your cheeks – until your whole head feels more relaxed. Then relax the back and sides of your neck, your throat, and the underside of your chin. When you find a tense place, enjoy the sensation of tension melting away. Move to your shoulders, your chest, your arms and hands, your belly, your back, your legs and feet, even your toes. Taste the feeling of relaxation, really feel it, enjoying it more and more, allowing it to nurture every part of your body. Stay with this experience until you feel it dissipating or diminishing.

Once again start from the top of your head and slowly proceed downwards as before. Think of the attention you are giving to each area of your body as a nurturing energy or light that can be absorbed by the skin. Allow your body to absorb this energy deeper below the surface of the skin like a sponge soaking up liquid. As you continue to scan down your body allow this energy to sink deeply into every organ and tissue of your body. Once you get to your toes, once again feel the whole of your body at the same time and continue the process of allowing it to be nurtured by the relaxation that is unfolding.

This cycle can be repeated as many times as desired. I recommend at least three times to start. In the beginning, each sweep should last between 5 to 7 minutes. You don't want to move too slowly since this will increase the likelihood of being distracted and cause you to forget where you were. Moving too fast won't allow you to feel what is happening.

When you decide to finish this exercise, once again allow yourself to experience your whole body feeling relaxed. As you prepare to end, continue to keep your eyes closed and with your mind's intention visualize what you will first see when you finally open your eyes. What will you see right in front of you? Try to see this as clearly as you can and as you visualize this try to maintain the feeling you are having from the relaxation created in your body. That is, continue to stay in touch with the felt sense of your being as you visualize what you anticipate seeing. There is no need to linger too long doing this (let's say around 20 – 30 seconds). Now gently open your eyes and see if you can retain the sensation in your body as you look out onto the world.

Most people will feel a strong pull to attend to the environment they find themselves in. This usually results in disconnecting from our bodies. By resisting this pull from the world and attempting to retain some of what you felt during the body scan you can begin to develop a resiliency in how to stay calm as you transition through the daily demands of living.

A Note On Using Your Attention

Throughout this guided exercise I have used the word "relax" loosely. You might even think it confusing to ask you to relax an area mentioned in order to become relaxed!

The key to realizing this relaxation is in how you deploy your attention. One aspect of paying attention is the directing of your focus to a specific target, whether it be your breath, a part of your body, an external object, etc. When directed to pay attention most people think of it in terms of "getting" or "fetching" something. There is the suggestion in this way of thinking that something must be grasped. This is not the kind of attention referred to here.

The idea of attending is more about how you allow your attention to rest on or in something. It is more about placing rather than acquiring. The Taoists refer to this as "wu-wei". Researchers refer to this as "passive volition". It is a paradoxical attitude of "doing by not doing". The idea here is to receive an impression.

We can translate this into an action of open curiosity. For example, when I scan my body as described in the above exercise, I contact each body part as a witnessing of its existence. That is, when I notice let's say my nose, I refrain from "seeing or making a picture" of my nose. Instead I notice what the nose actually feels like. Try not to describe it or label it but rather experience the sensation of having a nose. You can ask, "What's it like to have my nose?" Too often beginners will, by default, attempt to have an image and this often disconnects them from actually experiencing themselves.

Attending in this way is extremely powerful. Once you get used to it you begin to understand how, just by witnessing your body without judgment or analysis, it automatically shifts towards relaxing. The gateway to this is in the "feeling" of the sensation and not the "seeing" of the feature focused upon.

DIFFICULTIES RELAXING

It seems like relaxing should be the easiest thing to do. After all, when we are relaxed, we receive so many benefits. At the top of the list is that it is pleasurable and feels good. There is little or no effort involved and we generally are at ease. And yet, so many people report relaxing to be difficult.

Despite our best intentions we inevitably run into challenges and difficulties when attempting to establish a regular relaxation practice.

Most, if not all, difficulties are related to mind set. It is not that we can't relax. It is a natural ability. The problem is in how we think about relaxation, consciously or unconsciously. Our beliefs, attitudes and preferences are the main culprits in undermining our efforts. In this section some of the more popular difficulties will be examined.

NOT VALUING RELAXATION

Those of us living in the USA in particular are embedded in a cultural mindset that puts a priority on getting things done over allotting time to doing nothing. It is often heard that relaxing is "a waste of time". There is a constant pressure to accomplishing things and meeting goals. Relaxation is low on the list of value. It is considered frivolous and reserved for those moments that occur in between focusing on outcomes.

Holding to this belief obviously reduces the chances of ever practicing in the first place. We need to change this attitude and recognize that time spent relaxing is not a luxury but a necessity. We need to make relaxation a priority.

It is helpful to remind yourself about how relaxation can improve the way you get things done. It will improve your health and wellbeing and free up energy to work more effectively. Taking time out also gives a chance for more creative ways to address problems.

NOT HAVING TIME TO RELAX

Not having time to relax is related to not making it a priority. Many complain that their life is so busy that they can't squeeze relaxing into their schedules. Actually this is a question of stopping and giving yourself a moment to make a plan. Without planning the day we often feel out of control. We spend more time reacting to circumstances rather than being self-directed. The simple act of scheduling already establishes some relief.

In part, we want to build a situation that can allow us to create a habit of practice. To do so we need to consider what factors will encourage us to show up regularly to practice. So it is helpful to review what you do over the course of the day and see where a relaxation session can best fit. By best fit I mean that the circumstances and conditions for relaxing are reinforced and encouraged.

Most habits are triggered and maintained by cues that precede executing the habit. If I already have routines established I can couple the relaxation session to these routines. For instance, waking in the morning usually entails a sequence of self-care that has become highly routinized (washing up, brushing your teeth, eating a breakfast, etc.) Inserting your relaxation into this sequence can greatly increase doing your practice. Eating breakfast afterwards can also serve to reinforce your practice.

No matter where and when you choose to relax, it is important to be regular. Practicing at the same time each day will also reinforce actually doing it. This doesn't necessarily have to be based on clock time. For myself, rather than setting an actual time I select a place in a sequence as mentioned above. As soon as I awake I put water on my face and I sit down and do my practice. I don't insist on a time since I keep unusual hours for my work that can often keep me up late at night. As a result, there are days when I arise early and days when I arise late. Regardless of the time I wake up, I am always following the same sequence, which has become a habit.

"I Can't Relax"

Some people report that when they try to relax nothing happens. In other words, when they attempt to practice a technique, they do not experience what they expect to feel. Since our expectations aren't met, we think we aren't good at doing the exercise or that it doesn't work.

First of all, it is important to remember that relaxation is a process and that what we experience will change over time. When you first sit down to practice, it takes some time for all of you to settle. This is especially true if you have been busy with something else and now decide to stop. It is like shifting from one gear to another and the engine needs to rev down. Like a car, our body needs to shift gears.

By letting yourself "be", the body can come to rest. Rather than rejecting experiences of restlessness and being fidgety or tense, invite these sensations into your consciousness. Observe how they are actually manifesting without judgment. Giving space to these impressions usually results in their diminishing. [See Tracking Sensation Exercise].

Also examine your attitude about doing relaxation. If I bring to my practice a mindset that expects results or demands a specific outcome, the opposite is more likely to occur. You don't make yourself relax, you allow yourself to relax!

NEEDING TO STAY BUSY

A large segment of the population feel they need to stay busy. They exhibit a driven quality of being active almost to the point of mania. There is the fear that if they stop they will be overwhelmed by uncomfortable feelings and thoughts. Staying busy is a way to be distracted from such experiences. Under these circumstances, the goal is to prevent feelings of helplessness and despair from entering consciousness.

Maintaining such a stance drains our energy and is not very productive. Living life this way is scattering and exhausting. It also is not efficient and reduces the actual amount of work that is done.

To manage this, it may be necessary to take a bigger block of time off and have a mini-retreat. This could be where you set aside a morning or even a whole day and do something that you really want to do just for yourself.

Part of doing something exclusively for yourself is the consideration of confronting rather than avoiding those feelings of discomfort. You may need to seek support for dealing with them. Resolving such issues can greatly enhance your wellbeing and health.

A NOTE ON PUTTING
IT TOGETHER

The intention of this book is to provide a framework from which to develop some effective ways to cultivate deep relaxation. Briefly, relaxation is a natural process and requires regular practice to reap its benefits. It is easy to acquire and can be developed in small, incremental steps.

Think of practicing relaxation like exercising a set of muscles. With repetition the muscles get stronger and increases their ability to respond when needed. Without practice the muscles atrophy and aren't there when you need them. The practice of relaxation can be understood in a similar way.

Relaxation can be powerful all by itself. The rewards are immense, the benefits are felt almost immediately, and they accumulate with ongoing practice. As little as 20 minutes a day can yield profound outcomes.

So at the risk of being redundant, I wish to impress upon you that to really know how to relax and to take advantage of all that relaxation can offer requires a commitment to regular practice and applying the insights gained from such efforts.

As mentioned, the power of practicing to relax is that you get benefits from the very first time you try. It really comes down to the frequency of the effort you make. Each attempt to relax is like putting money in the bank and accruing interest. Each effort in and of itself may be small but it adds up. The more time put in, the more will be available to relax when needed.

However, it is important to consider how the use of relaxation can further other areas of your life.

The areas of healing, performance, creativity, and spirituality mentioned in the beginning of this book are all grounded in the ability to relax. There is so much information offered to us to better ourselves in each of these areas that it can be overwhelming and confusing.

One of my concerns as a trainer and coach is to drill down to the essential what must be learnt to achieve success. A few basic principles can generate most of what you need to be effective. There is always more and that should be the case. But how much you need to know to really get started should be limited. This is particularly the case because of the hectic schedules most of us follow today.

The point to keep in mind is that once you have acquired the ability to relax deeply, you are in a position to extend the experience beyond your practice sessions. The key to this is the frequency in which you connect with the experience of feeling relaxed.

To further assist your skill development, I am providing a complimentary strategy session that is designed to help you individualize your relaxation practice and start you on a program of life transformation. To schedule a session or to ask any question, please write to:

jeff@jeffkelton.com

Biographic Note

My career has now spanned more than 40 years, in which time I have straddled many different disciplines and pursuits. This has afforded me a unique perspective on the ways we heal, develop ourselves, achieve performance excellence, and align ourselves to the more transpersonal dimensions of our being.

I've worked in psychiatric hospitals and outpatient clinics with patients who experience severe emotional and mental disturbances. I've also worked with patients in my private practice who experience a wide range of milder concerns. I have had opportunities to provide training and consultations to business executives, Olympic athletes, USA

Military War Fighters and their families, USA diplomats, the Peace Corps, and performance artists as well as other creative people. My engagement with people has spanned the entire life cycle from early childhood to the elderly.

While developing myself "professionally", I have been a seeker of spiritual truth, which has included conducting scientific research on meditation practice for my PhD. Along the way I studied under a variety of spiritual masters in Yoga, Sufism, Taoism, and Shamanism. I have also studied and continue to train in Tai Chi Chuan and Qi Gong for 35 years.

My thirst for adventure and learning has included global travels to more than 40 countries and given me a perspective about how we live on this planet. From these sojourns I developed the GlobalWalkabouts™ Process, an experiential training that explores how to revive a Soulful connection to the Places we live in and on the Earth. Through this process I have guided leaders, truth seekers, and creatives to find and use their Inner GPS to navigate their journey in life. This approach has yielded outcomes beyond the expectations of those who enrolled and allowed participants to feel renewed, grounded and committed in their purpose while elevating their creativity and problem-solving capacities.

My life has been like the many streams that feed a major river. As I have continued my journey I have subsequently merged all these sources into a unique and powerful coaching practice. As a Life Coach I focus on helping my clients become fully awake to their lives and build the life they want which also serves the wellbeing of their community and the planet. This has proven to be the case for my clients whether they were a multi-million dollar business owner, solo entrepreneur, educator or medical practitioner, house wife/husband or artist.

Jeff Kelton, Ph.D.

www.JeffKelton.com

jeff@jeffkelton.com

APPENDIX

Following Sensation

(Kum Nye Relaxation, Part 1, 1978, p. 32)

Sit as relaxed and still as you can. Slowly let yourself become aware of any sensation or feeling-tone that arises. At the beginning you may have to remind yourself: remember! Follow whatever happens. You may feel a physical sensation or an emotion. The sensation does not need to be strong ... it may be light, even delicate. Be attuned to your inner ear. Trust the presence of your experience, and open yourself to it. Do this in whatever way you do it, without method or formulation. Whenever you feel a sensation or feeling-tone, allow it to continue as long as possible. Continue for fifteen to thirty minutes.

Stimulating feelings and expanding them is the basis of this exercise. In this way we learn to increase our enjoyment and appreciation of every aspect of living. Even a minute sensation can be increased, accumulated, and expanded until it flows throughout our bodies, and expands even beyond us to the surrounding world.

Kum Nye Relaxation, Part 1: Theory, Preparation, Massage by Tarthang Tulku. Dharma Publishing, 1978.

NOTES

NOTES

NOTES

NOTES

NOTES

NOTES

NOTES

NOTES

NOTES

NOTES

69516850R00052

Made in the USA
Columbia, SC
16 August 2019